How to Stand Still

A Beginners Guide to Meditation

By Mark Henry Scanlon

Introduction

Thank you for taking a moment to look through this small contribution to the practice of meditation.

When most people hear the word "meditation," they might picture monks or gurus sitting in impossible postures, radiating bliss and chasing enlightenment. But here, I want to invite you to think of meditation more simply, as a gateway to peace of mind, deeper understanding, and a source of inner inspiration.

This booklet was created with simplicity in mind. Inside, you will find a guided meditation you can follow at your own pace, along with practical techniques that support both physical and mental wellbeing. Whether you are completely new to meditation or just looking to reconnect with a sense of calm, this guide is here to meet you where you are.

You do not need any special background or beliefs, just a willingness to pause, breathe, and be present. I hope what you find here helps you create a small space of peace in your daily life, even if just for a few moments each day. In this guide, we will explore three simple types of meditation:

- **Stillness Meditation** – A practice to bring the body and mind into a calm, restful state. Over time, this practice can deepen, helping you experience layers of quiet and inner stillness.
- **Visualization Meditation** – A guided imagery practice that engages the imagination in a healing or inspiring way. It helps focus the mind and open the heart.
- **Mantra Meditation** – A method of repeating a word, phrase, or sound to anchor your awareness and settle mental activity.

I created this guide based on what helped me and the people I work with. Meditation has supported me through stress, helped me reconnect with my body, and guided me toward a clearer, calmer mind. I believe everyone can benefit from it, not as something mystical, but as something practical.

Preparation

"Everything begins and ends in stillness."

How do We Prepare for Meditation?

Before we begin to meditate, it helps to take a few moments to prepare, not just physically, but mentally and emotionally as well. This preparation allows us to be more relaxed, more focused, and more present.

1. Choose a Calm Space

When you are first starting out, it is helpful to find a place where you will not be disturbed. It does not need to be completely silent, but you should feel at ease and safe in the space. Meditation can sometimes bring up unexpected emotions, so having a calm environment can help you feel grounded and supported.

2. Find a Comfortable Posture

The body must feel comfortable, especially during longer sessions. Even a small discomfort can grow and make it difficult to focus. You do not need to sit cross-legged; a chair is perfectly fine. But try not to lean on the backrest. Your posture should feel both **relaxed and**

alert. Too relaxed, and you might fall asleep. Too tense, and you will not be able to settle.

3. Let Go of Expectations

One of the most important things to bring into meditation is nothing at all. Do not go in expecting anything, not peace, not insight, not a perfect experience. Hoping or grasping for something often gets in the way. Just allow the practice to unfold as it is. Let it be what it is today.

4. Settle the Body and Mind

Some people find it helpful to stretch, walk gently, or perform a simple movement practice before sitting. Personally, I often use Qigong to settle my energy and bring myself into the present. The past can try to pull you back, and the mind loves to imagine the future. Movement, breath, or a moment of pause can help bring you into the *now*, the only place where meditation truly happens.

Types of Meditation

"Meditation and concentration are the way to a life of serenity." – Baba Ram Dass spiritual teacher and author of Be Here Now

Stillness Meditation

Stillness meditation is just what it sounds like, to be still, to be unmoved, and to be unconcerned. It is easy to understand in theory, but far harder to truly practice.

Anyone can sit still physically. But bringing the mind into stillness, that is where the real challenge lies. Thoughts, emotions, memories, and distractions all rise up the moment we pause. That is why this practice takes patience, and why it can be so powerful.

The Breath as an Anchor

One of the simplest and most reliable ways to help the mind become still is to focus on your breathing Gently turn your attention to the act of breathing itself. Feel the air move in and out of your body. You do not need to breathe in any special way, just notice it.

If your mind starts to wander, try **counting your breaths**. Start at one and count each inhale or exhale. I often suggest aiming for **one hundred breaths** to help calm the mind. But do not worry about the number. Go for as long as you need, some days it may take just a few moments, other times longer. Over time, you will become more aware of how your mind and body are feeling.

When the Mind Becomes Still

Once the breath has calmed the body and the mind begins to quiet down, you will notice a shift. You are not trying to do anything. You are not chasing thoughts or pushing them away. You are simply being. Unmoved. Present. Still.

This is the heart of stillness meditation, not doing anything, but simply being present in the moment.

Visualization Meditation

Like stillness meditation, visualization is simple to explain, but harder to truly practice. Having roots in many different places, in terms of what I will teach you here is a simple, barebones approach that is accessible to anyone. Generally, to perform this kind of meditation we engage the imagination, the more vivid you can imagine, the more you can engage your thoughts depending on the goal of your meditation, the more you will get out of the session. When I tend to teach this form of meditation, I act as a narrator, guiding the students through the visualization until they no longer need me.

Nature-Based Visualizations

These are some of the easiest and most effective to begin with. Nature has a calming effect on the mind.

- **A peaceful forest** — walking slowly through trees, listening to birdsong, feeling the soft earth under your feet.

- **A quiet beach** — the sound of waves, the warmth of the sun, the softness of sand between your toes.

- **A flowing river or waterfall** — letting its sound wash away your stress, feeling refreshed as you breathe.

These help to calm the nervous system and create a deep sense of peace.

Light and Energy Visualizations

These are especially powerful for healing or spiritual meditation.

- **A glowing light** in your chest or hands, growing brighter with each breath.

- **Breathing in white or golden light**, filling your whole body with peace, warmth, or healing.

- **Cleansing light** washing through your body, clearing tension or negative energy as it moves.

These types are great for Qigong and energy work too.

Spiritual or Symbolic Visualizations

For those with a spiritual background, you can imagine powerful symbols or scenes that carry deep meaning for you.

- **Standing in front of a great mountain** representing wisdom or strength.

- **Walking through a gate** into a sacred or safe place.

- **Meeting a spiritual guide**, angel, saint, or just a sense of loving presence, letting them speak peace into your heart.

Emotional and Inner Work Visualizations

These are helpful for self-discovery and emotional healing.

- **Visualizing a younger version of yourself,** offering comfort and compassion.

- **Letting go of emotional burdens**, imagining them as stones you set down or clouds that drift away.

- **Creating a safe space** in your mind where you can return whenever you feel overwhelmed.

Mantra Meditation

Mantra meditation is the practice of repeating a word, phrase, or sound to help focus the mind. The repeated word is called a *mantra*, and its main purpose is to serve as an anchor, something the mind can gently rest on instead of drifting into thoughts or distractions.

The mantra can be spoken out loud, whispered, or silently repeated in your mind. What matters most is the rhythm and repetition, which creates a calming effect and helps bring your attention back whenever it wanders.

Some people use spiritual or traditional mantras, but in a more general or secular approach, it can be any word or phrase that feels grounding or meaningful to you. For example, someone might repeat the word "peace," "relax," or "breathe." Others might use phrases like "I am calm" or "Let go."

You do not need to believe in anything specific for mantra meditation to work, it is about using the sound or phrase to still the mind, reduce mental chatter, and enter a more peaceful state of awareness.

If you notice your thoughts wandering, simply return to the mantra. Over time, this practice can help you build focus, calm your emotions, and stay present.

Challenges of Meditation

*"The practice isn't about being perfect — it's about returning.
Again and again, gently and patiently. That is the meditation."*

When it comes to meditation, there are some common challenges that almost everyone faces at some point. Knowing them ahead of time can help you navigate the experience more gently and with less frustration.

- **Maintaining Focus**
  One of the most important skills in meditation is the ability to stay focused. But ironically, it is also one of the hardest things to do, especially in the beginning. The mind naturally wanders. It jumps to the past, races into the future, or starts thinking about dinner. This is normal. What matters is not *stopping* the wandering, but gently noticing it, and returning your attention, again and again, to the breath, the body, or your chosen anchor.

- **Staying Relaxed While Focused**
  Focus is important, but so is relaxation. Too much effort can make you tense. You might find yourself "trying" to meditate, clenching your jaw or furrowing your brow without realizing it. Meditation is not about forcing the mind to behave; it is about *allowing*. The balance is in being alert without strain. This is why posture and breath awareness are so helpful, they teach you to be calm and awake at the same time.

- **Impatience or Restlessness**

  Many people get frustrated when "nothing happens." But meditation is not about getting somewhere fast. It is more like growing a tree, slow, natural, and subtle. Progress is often invisible at first, but over time, something beautiful and grounded begins to grow within you.

- **Emotional Surfacing**

  Sometimes sitting quietly allows buried emotions to rise, sadness, anxiety, anger. This is not a sign that something's wrong. In fact, it is a sign of healing. Let the feelings come and go like waves. If it becomes too overwhelming, take a break, ground yourself, or return to a more physical form of meditation like walking or Qigong.

- **Doubt or Self-Criticism**

  It is common to wonder: "Am I doing this right?" The truth is, there is no perfect meditation. Each session will be different. Some will feel peaceful. Others will feel difficult. What matters is showing up and staying open, not performing or achieving.

Awareness Meditation

A Pilgrimage of Awareness

"Open the door of awareness and know you."

The Outer World

"Where we interact, react and perform."

Before we turn inward, we must take in the world around us, this outer world. Let your eyes be closed, or gently lowered, and bring your attention to the space you are in. Feel the air on your skin, is it cool or warm? Is there movement or stillness? Notice the sounds that reach you, do not try to name them, just listen with polite interest and allow each sound to rise and fall, come and go. Some may be soft, others loud or distant. Just continue to listen, like a witness, with no need to judge or reach.

Become aware of the sensation of where you are sitting. The contact points of your body, supported by the chair or the ground. Let yourself feel that support. Let the body be held. Then imagine the room around you, the walls, floor and ceiling. You do not need to see it clearly, just a soft awareness of the space. The outside world is still there, but for now, you do not need to respond to it.

With each breath, the outer world begins to fade into the background. The edges soften. You can now begin to withdraw from what is outside and gently move within.

The Inner World

"Where we observe and feel."

As we begin with a simple scan of the body, I invite you to turn your awareness inward. Let go of the outside world, its distractions, its demands and begin the slow journey into your own, inner world.

Imagine you are standing beneath a warm shower. The sensation of water flowing over you is your awareness, soothing, washing, easing its way through the body. Let it start at the crown of your head.

Feel it flow across your scalp, your forehead, softening the muscles around your eyes. Let it trickle over your temples, those spaces where thoughts tend to gather. Follow the cheeks to the jaw, even your tongue, let go of any clenching. Let the jaw hang loose, the tongue to rest gently in the mouth. Your awareness melts into the muscles and bones beneath, as though the skull begins to breath and soften.

Let this gentle stream now pour over your shoulders, that place we often carry the invisible weight of life. It is as if we hold the weight of the world there. But here, in this moment, you can release that burden. Let go.

Awareness now travels down your arms, flowing like water through each joint and muscle. Through your elbows, wrists, and all the way to your fingertips. Each finger releases, unwinds, until they are simply resting, no longer gripping anything.

Now bring your attention to your chest, the space that rises and falls with each breath. This is the centre of our tension when anxious, the tightness that speaks when words cannot. Let yourself feel the natural rhythm of the breath, and allow the muscles of your chest to relax as the breath flows easier and deeper.

Let your awareness travel to your back, the strong yet sensitive pillar that supports you. From the upper back to the mid-spine, slowly down to the lower back, follow the length of the spine as if tracing a river. So much is held here, responsibility, effort, history. And yet, now, there is space to release. Let the spine align itself without force and the muscles find their natural state, without tension.

Feel the base of your spine, the hips, this foundation that holds your posture and often holds our past as well. Let it all be soften. The pelvis, tailbone, grounding you gently.

Now bring your awareness to the hips and pelvis, the seat of your balance and stability. Notice any tension that may be tucked away here, perhaps from long days, stored emotions, or simply the posture of life. Let your awareness move like warm water through the joints, muscles and bones, softening, loosening, easing any tightness.

Allow this wave of awareness to flow into your thighs, strong and steady pillars that support you. These large muscles do so much without thanks. Allow them now to rest, to release. From the tops of your thighs down to your knees, let the warmth of awareness continue, relaxing every inch along the way.

The knees, those remarkable joints that bend and bear our journey through life. So often they carry more than just our weight, sometimes they carry fear or anticipation. Let them soften now. Let go of effort. Let go of holding.

Allow the awareness to move down through your calves, muscles that work with every step you take, often unnoticed. Feel them ease, feel them unwind. The ankles, too, they adjust constantly for balance and direction. Let them settle, let them find stillness.

And now, finally arrive at your feet, the foundation of your body, the contact point between you and the earth. So much of our experience travels through the feet, yet we rarely give them our attention. So, take a moment here. Bring your awareness into the soles of your feet, the heels, the arches, the balls of the feet, and all ten toes.

Imagine now your entire body, from head to toe, bathed in this warm, flowing awareness. Follow that stillness deeper as you breath, and let every exhale release more tension, more weight, more thought.

There is nowhere else you need to be right now. There is nothing else you need to do. Simply remain here, in stillness and presence, aware and relaxed.

The Mind, our Deeper World

"Built from the past and grown with the future."

I want to invite you now to go deeper, beyond the inner world of the body, to the mind, our consciousness where the past resides, a place of memories, both good and bad. But just as the mind imagines, these memories are simply records of where you have come from, the experiences that have built you piece by piece into the person you are now. We do not stay within the walls of the past, but visit from time to time, to remember or draw courage.

Now we look at the future, just as the past is a record, the future is just imagined. For as much as we plan, we imagine or know for certainty what is to come, the future is not real and once it is we call it the present, a gift we wait for.

The Still Point, the Centre of the Self

"Where we rest."

Let us go deeper, beyond thought, beyond memory and imagination. At the heart, the very centre is a quiet space, a place untouched by the past, untroubled by the future. A still point. It is not a thought, or feeling, but a place of simple awareness, where we rest. In this place you are not a story, with a name, a role or plans and a past. But you are simply being.

Rest here for a moment, nothing to change, or fix, just be still. If thoughts arise here, just observe them as they pass you by and remain still, unmoved by what might come up.

This is the heart, the centre of your most inner world, the quiet behind the noise, a place you can always return too.

Return to the Outer World

"Every breath is its own journey."

You have journeyed deep, from the outer world of space and vibration, to the inner world of the body and mind. And finally sat still at the centre of your being. Now, without rushing, begin the journey back. Allow your awareness to begin expanding, feel the breath once again as your awareness moves throughout the body, like a calm, glowing light at the centre of your body reaching out in all directions as your awareness returns.

Continue to feel the light of awareness fill the room again, what sounds do you hear, can you feel the air on your body.

Take a slow, deep, breath in, and allow it to leave the body carry that light of awareness into the room. You are back in the outer world, but changed, more aware and grounded. More you.

"This place of stillness is always within you, with just a breath, just a moment, you can return."

Reflection

What did you notice today? How did your body feel? What stood out in your mind? There are no wrong answers, only honest reflections. This is how we learn to listen more deeply to ourselves.

Meditation is a personal experience, a personal journey. In my own practice, I often keep a notebook nearby to jot down thoughts, feelings, or moments that stood out. Over time, these reflections become part of the journey too, showing where you have been, and gently guiding where you are going.

Printed in Dunstable, United Kingdom